Love Finds Its Way Home

Surviving Trauma, Finding Strength, Embracing Love

I0559022

By: Debra Staff

Author's Note & Dedication

This book is a labour of love, a testament to survival, healing, & the quiet courage that blooms in the face of trauma. Every page holds fragments of my story, the lives of those I have loved, & the lessons learned through grief, joy, & transformation.

To Pops, my Labrador Retriever, whose unwavering loyalty & gentle spirit taught me the meaning of unconditional love, thank you. To Sebast, my spirited Cocker Poodle, whose curiosity & trust remind me daily that life continues to offer light, thank you. You both have shown me that love never ends - it simply finds new ways to shine.

To every woman who has endured, who has survived herself, & who continues to rise despite the weight of the past: this is for you. May these words offer comfort, strength, & reassurance that your courage matters, that your pain does not define you, & that your light will always find its way home.

To the friends, family, & kind souls who have walked beside me in moments of darkness & in times of celebration: your presence, patience, & understanding have been priceless gifts. Thank you for believing in me when I doubted myself, & for holding space for the parts of me that needed to heal.

This book is more than a collection of reflections, poems, & quotes. It is a reminder that love, in all its forms, is eternal; that strength is often quiet, yet unstoppable; & that the human heart, even when fractured, has the power to mend, to grow, & to shine brighter than ever before.

May every reader find solace here, a spark of courage, & a whisper of hope. May these pages remind you that even after the darkest storms, love finds its way home.

With all my heart & gratitude,

Debs

Copyright Page

© 2025 Debs Staff

Table Of Contents

Part One
Origins of a Storm

I had a loving childhood. My dad sat by my bed through the long nights, listening for the whistle of my asthma, steady hands ready to help me breathe again. He never once left me to face it alone. And my mum, she was love in motion - warm arms, kind eyes, a voice that could calm any storm. She filled the house with care, made even ordinary days feel safe. She fought her own battles quietly, but always made sure I felt seen & cherished. She is still my drive, my heartbeat, my why.

When I was young, that sense of safety was taken. Someone who should have cared for me caused harm instead. The truth came out years later, but justice never truly did. I was heard, but not protected. Believed, but not saved. That was my first lesson in how the world can turn away from what it does not want to face.

In the years that followed, I found a home with Derry, my foster mum, my steady light in the years after. She was safety restored. The proof that love can begin again even when trust feels impossible. Still, the system gave me labels instead of understanding. They called it personality disorder, depression, anxiety, instability. Later, they called it bipolar. I was too young to know what any of it really meant, only that I had lost control of my own story.

Through everything, my mum stayed my anchor. Her love never wavered, even as life kept testing us both. Then came the night everything changed. I dropped her home in the early hours. Her last words were, "I love you, Debs." I can still hear her breath, soft, final, unforgettable. I knew something was wrong. I called for help that morning, but no one came until the night. By then she was gone.

They called it accidental. A mix of medicines that never should have been prescribed together, a mistake that took her life & left our truth buried beneath official words. The report closed the door. The silence that followed was unbearable. My sister & I fought for answers, but the systems we trusted turned their faces away. The people meant to protect us hid behind their titles & procedures. That was the day my faith in authority broke, but not my faith in love.

Because love is what Mum left behind, & that love became the pulse that carried me through everything that followed.

In the weeks & months afterward, I carried grief like a living thing. It rested in my chest, sat heavy on my shoulders, whispered in my ears at every quiet moment. The world seemed too loud, too fast, too careless. Yet within me, there was a flicker of something stronger than despair. I clung to memories of Mum, the soft laugh that rose even in the hardest days, the gentle hands that soothed without words. I began to understand that love is not a possession, it's a pulse, a rhythm that travels beyond what eyes can see.

School became a blur. Faces changed, names faded, lessons felt hollow. People spoke & I heard only fragments, words that landed in a fog of grief & fear. Teachers tried to help, but no one could reach the hollow that had formed inside me. I learned to hide, to bend, to become a shadow that passed through hallways unnoticed. It was easier to vanish than to explain the chaos within. & yet, the memories of Mum stayed vivid, a compass pointing me back to safety even when the world felt lost.

Then came Pops, though I didn't know it yet. A golden light, a heartbeat on four legs, who would become a guardian, a teacher, a reminder that joy is still possible. Even in the darkest hours, he would be the proof that love can survive the storm. And later Sebast joined us, small, curious, softness, a bridge between the pain of the past & the hope of the future. In them, I found fragments of home, reminders that the world could still be gentle, that loyalty & devotion are not just human traits.

But life did not pause for healing. Hospital visits, misdiagnoses, labels multiplied. I became familiar with doors closing, voices arguing over my truth, papers signed without understanding, interventions that missed the heart of the pain. I learned to carry resilience quietly, to walk softly through corridors that smelled of antiseptic & fear, to whisper Mum's name like a prayer that no one else could hear. I learned that love can survive neglect, that patience can endure uncertainty, that even when your world is fractured, fragments of hope remain.

By the time I was sixteen, I knew the shape of absence intimately. I had tasted the bitterness of injustice & the hollow echo of unanswered questions. & yet, love kept returning. From Mum, from Derry, from Pops & Sebast. It was not the love of convenience, or ease, or fairness - it was the love that persists even when every system, every rule, every expectation turns away. That love became my anchor, my light, my reason to continue moving through a world that often seemed determined to forget me.

I realized early that survival is not passive. It demands courage, the stubbornness to keep walking, the refusal to let labels define the story of your heart. My childhood was fractured, yes, but it was also filled with moments of grace, of laughter, of tender hands & quiet reassurance. Those fragments became the foundation I built upon, the seeds of strength that would carry me forward. though storms would come again & again, I knew that love always finds its way home.

Part Two
The Loss of Self

After the first storm, the world looked different. The safety I once knew had vanished, replaced by a quiet terror that lived in every shadow, every echo, every passing glance. My body remembered pain before my mind fully understood it. I felt it in my chest, in the sharp ache behind my ribs, in the trembling that would not stop even when I told myself I was safe. Grief had become a companion, a heavy, living weight that pressed me into corners, whispered doubts, and rewrote every expectation I once had of life.

I stopped trusting easily. Even those who meant well were filtered through the lens of survival. I measured every smile, every gesture, every word, questioning intention, meaning, & honesty. My heart became cautious, guarded, armored in ways that were invisible yet palpable. At school, I learned to fade. My voice became quiet, my body moved in careful rhythms to avoid drawing attention, and I watched as life continued for everyone else while I struggled to remember who I was beneath the shadows.

Therapy came too late to prevent the cracks, but not too late to start filling them. Some sessions offered validation, some left me raw, exposed, & more aware of how fractured I had become. I was told that identity is fluid, that trauma reshapes perception, that survival requires adjustments that may feel strange to the outside world. I nodded, absorbing each word, but I also carried skepticism because I knew words were easy, but living in a body that remembered every violation, every betrayal, every lost night was different. Reality was heavier than theory, pain heavier than advice, & my sense of self had become a puzzle of missing pieces I was not allowed to see.

The labels multiplied. They piled up in files, in appointments, in casual conversations that did not understand the gravity of my lived experience. Personality disorder, bipolar, depression, anxiety, emotional instability. I read the words, repeated them to myself, tried to make them fit the story I thought I should be telling, but nothing aligned. I was more than the sum of diagnoses. I was the echo of my mother's love, the pulse of my father's care, the flicker of light that Pops brought when I collapsed into the silence of my room. Labels were insufficient. They were paper shields in a world that demanded more than explanations.

Trust was the currency I had lost. I learned early that it is fragile, that systems meant to protect can fail spectacularly, that people sometimes act according to convenience rather than justice. I approached life cautiously, testing, probing, measuring reactions to ensure my vulnerability would not be exploited. Yet in this caution, there was also a loneliness that seeped into the marrow of my bones. Loneliness that whispered, "You are unseen, you are unheard, you are alone." It was relentless. The nights became my enemies, quiet hours stretching into landscapes of memories that refused to rest.

Pops arrived during these years, a Labrador reminder that devotion does not betray, that love can exist without condition, without agenda, without demand. His tail wagged like an invitation to return to joy. His eyes reflected a universe that understood the language of my pain without a single word spoken. He reminded me that healing, though slow, is possible. Sebast, arriving later with soft paws & curiosity, added laughter, mischief, and lessons in living fully even after sorrow. In them, I found fragments of what I had lost in myself, glimpses of a self that could trust, play, & feel without fear.

Yet the world around me did not pause for my healing. Adults made decisions on my behalf, their words carrying authority, their actions often misaligned with care. Hospital visits became punctuations of uncertainty, appointments a reminder that people interpreted me rather than understood me. Misdiagnoses piled upon misdiagnoses, a testament to the struggle of navigating life while burdened with labels that rarely captured my truth. I learned to hold the fragments of my identity close, secret, and sacred, revealing only when absolutely necessary.

The loss of self is not sudden. It is a gradual erosion, a peeling away of trust, confidence, innocence, & clarity. It is nights spent questioning whether your thoughts belong to you or to the trauma that shaped you. It is mornings when the reflection in the mirror feels unfamiliar, a stranger's face staring back with eyes that have seen too much. It is the dissonance between who you were before and the survival mechanisms you adopted to endure. Every day became a balancing act, a negotiation with shadows, a reminder that life is both fragile & resilient simultaneously.

I learned to seek love where it was real, genuine, and loyal. I discovered that not every connection is safe, not every word is honest, not every hand extended is steady. But with Pops & Sebast, with the memory of Mum, I found a framework of security that allowed me to breathe. I realized that healing does not require permission, that strength is built in quiet moments of consistency, & that self-respect is cultivated when boundaries are maintained with intention & care.

As adolescence progressed, my awareness of loss deepened. Friendships shifted, alliances changed, and I discovered that people are often inconsistent. Some who seemed steadfast vanished when I needed them most, their absence amplifying the feeling that the world is a place where love is fragile and fleeting. I grieved for these vanished relationships, mourning not only the loss of companionship but also the betrayal of expectations. I became more attuned to energy, motives, and the quiet signals that guide survival when the heart is vulnerable.

School achievements became a mask, a measure of control in a world where so much felt uncontrollable. I excelled academically, not for the accolades, but to prove to myself that competence exists within me despite the chaos. I wrote journals, captured memories, and created stories that gave my internal world form. Writing became a sanctuary, a space where my voice could be unbroken, where I could make sense of a reality that often-defied comprehension. The act of creation became a lifeline, a thread weaving together the fragments of self that trauma had attempted to fracture.

I remember nights lying awake while Pops rested beside me, feeling his warmth against my skin, and recognizing that even in silence, love communicates its presence. I would whisper to him my fears, my regrets, my doubts, and he would listen without judgment, without expectation, offering only the pure, unwavering love that animals are uniquely capable of giving. These quiet exchanges taught me that even when human understanding falters, connection is possible, & that trust can be rebuilt incrementally with patience, persistence, & presence.

By the end of these formative years, I understood that the loss of self is not permanent. It is a state of suspension, a shadow waiting to be illuminated by awareness, patience, & deliberate acts of reclaiming identity. Recovery is not linear. There are setbacks, moments of doubt, hours of despair, but also breakthroughs, flashes of clarity, & incremental victories. Each step toward self-reclamation is an affirmation that trauma cannot permanently define the essence of a person, that love, loyalty, & resilience can reassemble a fractured self.

The presence of Pops & Sebast, along with the enduring lessons from Mum, became my anchors in this rebuilding. They reminded me that safety can exist, that joy is attainable, & that identity is not solely shaped by external circumstances. In witnessing their lives, their consistency, & their devotion, I began to understand that selfhood is an active creation. It requires intention, courage, & the willingness to confront fear while nurturing hope.

I started to recognize moments of agency, however small. Choosing to speak, to write, to act in alignment with my values, which became revolutionary. I began to notice that even amid instability, the seeds of self-trust, independence, & authenticity could flourish. Survival had taught me vigilance, but healing taught me discernment. I discovered that the capacity to love, to laugh, & to be present resides within, waiting to be nurtured by deliberate choices & compassionate self-engagement.

The loss of self is not the absence of identity, but the postponement of its full realization. It is a pause between what was & what can become. Through the dark corridors of adolescence & early adulthood, I learned to navigate the shadow, to honor the grief, & to celebrate the fragments of strength that emerged even in moments of despair. I realized that trauma shapes without wholly defining, & that identity, though challenged, remains capable of regeneration.

By the time I reached adulthood, I had become familiar with the duality of existence. The world is capable of harm & care, cruelty & tenderness, loss & restoration. I had experienced profound pain, betrayal, & injustice, but I had also experienced unwavering love, loyalty, & light. I carried the memory of Mum, the quiet guidance of Pops, & the gentle joy of Sebast as living reminders that selfhood is resilient, adaptable, & capable of profound growth.

Every moment of connection, whether with humans or animals, became a lesson in reclamation. Every step toward self-expression, every choice made with integrity, every instance of asserting boundaries reinforced the identity that trauma had attempted to fracture. I learned that my voice, my presence, & my perspective matter. They are part of the blueprint for reclaiming a life defined not solely by suffering but by endurance, authenticity, & the relentless pursuit of love, joy, & belonging.

In this reclamation, I discovered the enduring truth: love is both a salve & a compass. It guides recovery, nourishes resilience, & illuminates the path towards selfhood. Trust, once broken, can be repaired incrementally. Identity, once threatened, can be rebuilt through acts of courage, reflection, & consistent engagement with one's own needs. Healing is not immediate, but it is inevitable when met with intention, patience, & support from both seen & unseen sources of love.

The loss of self, though harrowing, became the foundation upon which I could rebuild. Each challenge faced, each obstacle overcome, each quiet victory contributed to a growing understanding that identity is neither fragile nor fixed. It is a living, evolving force capable of surviving storms, reclaiming space, & embracing life fully once more. Through grief, love, reflection, & deliberate action, I began to emerge not merely as a survivor, but as a conscious architect of my own being.

Part Three
Awakening Strength

Strength is not loud, not brash, not always visible. It grows quietly in the spaces between fear & courage, in the moments where the world has demanded we bend but we rise instead. After years of loss, confusion, & fractured identity, I began to notice the subtle ways resilience begins to take root. It is not an immediate transformation, not a sudden epiphany. It is a process, gentle & deliberate, built from persistence, awareness, & the quiet decision to choose life, even when life feels uncertain, unkind, or unforgiving.

The first moments of awakening came as whispers. A sense of self returning, a pulse of confidence beneath the layers of doubt. I began to notice my body in ways I had neglected, to recognize the voice in my mind that reminded me of my capacity to endure. Each morning became a subtle challenge, an invitation to rise, to move through the day with intention, to affirm that I mattered, that my experience mattered, & that my existence had inherent value. These early victories were invisible to most, but they were monumental to me. They signified the reclamation of a self that trauma had tried to erase.

I learned that strength is not measured by the absence of fear. It is measured by persistence, by the courage to step forward even when doubt whispers loudly, when anxiety tightens its grip, when the shadows of the past seek to remind us of every time we were silenced, diminished, or dismissed. Each step I took toward self-assertion became a declaration: I will not shrink to accommodate the discomfort of others. I will not dim my light to make those around me comfortable. I will rise, slowly, deliberately, & unapologetically.

Support came in many forms. Some human, some animal, some entirely intangible. Pops reminded me that loyalty is steadfast, that love is consistent, that presence alone can soothe the deepest unrest. Sebast taught me joy, spontaneity, & the grace of living fully in a single moment. Friends who stayed, even when it was inconvenient or uncomfortable for them, became anchors of validation, reflecting my worth when I struggled to see it myself. And in the quiet moments of reflection, I discovered the inner dialogue I had long silenced: the voice that always believed, that had always hoped, that had always been waiting for me to listen.

Strength also required confrontation. Confronting boundaries I had ignored, confronting patterns that no longer served me, confronting memories that had been buried but never healed. I realized that avoidance prolongs pain, that silence allows fear to grow, & that reclamation requires acknowledgment, not denial. Every moment of facing what once terrified me became an act of courage. Every decision to speak, to act, to claim my space in the world was a declaration that I existed not merely as a survivor, but as a living, active, conscious being.

The process of awakening strength is both internal & external. Internally, it requires self-awareness, mindfulness, & radical acceptance of one's own imperfections. Externally, it requires advocacy, presence, & the courage to establish boundaries that honor self-respect without alienating compassion. I discovered that strength is often mistaken for aggression, resilience for stubbornness, confidence for arrogance, but true power is far more subtle. It manifests in patience, consistency, empathy, reflection, & the unyielding decision to continue despite uncertainty.

I began to explore practices that nurtured this growth. Journaling, meditation, physical movement, moments of solitude, creative expression, & deliberate acts of self-care. Each became a thread woven into the fabric of my emerging strength. I wrote letters I never sent, allowed tears to fall without shame, & learned to breathe deeply into spaces of discomfort. I discovered that presence matters: being present for myself, acknowledging my own needs, listening to my intuition, & refusing to dismiss the quiet messages my body & mind were sending.

Empowerment became the cornerstone of awakening strength. It was not the loud, performative kind, but the quiet, relentless assertion that my voice, my choice, my perspective, & my body were my own. Saying no became a radical act. Choosing solitude when necessary became a statement of self-preservation. Asking for help, once terrifying, became a demonstration of courage. I recognized that strength is not isolation, but connection: knowing when to reach out, when to hold space for others, & when to honor the sacred sanctuary of one's own presence.

As I embraced this awakening, I noticed shifts in relationships. Connections that had been transactional or conditional faded, making space for authentic bonds rooted in mutual respect, shared values, & genuine affection. I became attuned to the energy of people around me, learning to identify those who supported growth versus those who reinforced patterns of doubt, shame, or suppression. These discernments were uncomfortable but necessary, for strength cannot flourish in environments that thrive on diminishment.

Moments of reflection revealed patterns I had internalized from trauma. The belief that I must prove worthiness, that love is conditional, that vulnerability is weakness. Each realization was a seed of transformation. By consciously replacing these beliefs with affirmations of inherent value, self-compassion, & the legitimacy of my emotions, I slowly dismantled the internalized limitations that had hindered growth. Strength, I discovered, is as much about dismantling old narratives as it is about building new ones.

I learned to find joy in small victories: completing tasks I once avoided, expressing thoughts that once trembled in silence, honoring boundaries that once felt impossible. These micro-triumphs accumulated into momentum, creating a reservoir of confidence I could draw upon in moments of doubt. Strength became not just reactive, but proactive: choosing actions aligned with values, creating conditions conducive to growth, & actively seeking opportunities for empowerment in both the mundane & the extraordinary.

My body, once a battlefield, became a source of insight & reassurance. Movement, rest, nourishment, & gentle care became acts of reclaiming agency. I listened to aches & fatigue not as punishment but as communication, a reminder to honor my limits while celebrating resilience. Every stretch, every step, every conscious breath reinforced the message: I am present, I am capable, & I am reclaiming sovereignty over my being.

Awakening strength also demanded patience. Growth is not linear. There are setbacks, moments of doubt, days where the past feels overwhelmingly present. But even in these moments, I began to recognize the subtle victories: surviving the night without panic, speaking truth without shame, feeling joy without guilt. Patience is not passive; it is active endurance, acknowledgment of progress even when it is incremental, & trust in the unfolding of one's own evolution.

Self-expression became a cornerstone of resilience. Writing, art, movement, even fashion, became declarations of existence, markers of identity, & tools for processing experiences. Creativity offered a channel for energy previously confined to survival, transforming it into insight, clarity, & emotional release. Each creation, no matter how small, reinforced the message that I am capable of contributing, of producing beauty, & of transforming struggle into empowerment.

Spiritual awareness emerged as another anchor. Whether in moments of silent reflection, meditation, or observation of the natural world, I felt a connection to a force larger than myself. This awareness offered perspective, reminding me that my challenges, while deeply personal, are part of the broader human experience. Strength, I realized, is both intimate & universal: personal fortitude intertwined with the shared capacity to endure, heal, & rise.

By embracing awareness, agency, empowerment, patience, creativity, & spiritual insight, my strength began to radiate outward. Decisions were made with clarity, boundaries enforced with compassion, & relationships cultivated with intentionality. I no longer sought permission to exist fully. I claimed space, honored needs, & approached life with a quiet confidence rooted in survival, reflection, & deliberate growth.

Resilience became habitual. Small actions repeated consistently created momentum that carried me through challenges that once felt insurmountable. Awareness of progress reinforced commitment to continued growth. I understood that awakening strength is not a final destination but a lifelong journey, one that requires vigilance, self-compassion, & deliberate engagement with the world while honoring internal truths.

Pops & Sebast remained companions, not merely pets, but teachers in resilience, patience, & joy. Their presence reminded me that love can exist without demand, that connection can be healing, & that life offers moments of light even in the midst of darkness. Observing them navigate the world with instinctive confidence encouraged me to trust intuition, to honor emotion, & to act decisively when alignment with values was required.

By the end of this awakening, I recognized that strength is multidimensional. It encompasses emotional endurance, physical fortitude, relational awareness, intellectual clarity, & spiritual presence. Strength is both the capacity to withstand hardship & the willingness to embrace vulnerability. It is the courage to act despite fear, to love despite past wounds, & to rise repeatedly even when the world has tried to convince you that rising is impossible.

Through the deliberate cultivation of these qualities, I became an architect of my own resilience. No longer defined solely by past trauma, I began to operate from a foundation of self-awareness, integrity, compassion, & intentionality. I reclaimed identity, agency, & power, understanding that the journey toward strength is ongoing, evolving, & rich with discovery.

Every challenge faced in the past became a teacher, every moment of perseverance a testament to capacity, every connection honored a source of support. Strength awakened not in isolation, but through engagement, reflection, & recognition of the profound interplay between internal resolve & external circumstance. In this awakening, I discovered that survival is the precursor to flourishing, & that the conscious cultivation of resilience transforms the remnants of pain into a living, vibrant testament to the human spirit.

Part Four
Love Finds Its Way

Love is not always immediate, not always obvious, not always safe. Sometimes it comes quietly, in moments you least expect, in places you never thought to look, & in ways that challenge your understanding of yourself. After the storms of trauma, the painstaking work of reclaiming strength, the conscious rebuilding of self, love often feels like both a risk & a reward. It is simultaneously fragile & fierce, tentative & transformative. Learning to recognize it, to welcome it, & to nurture it is a journey that requires courage, patience, & openness to vulnerability.

The first whispers of love began not with another person, but within myself. After years of survival, I realized that the most radical act is often self-love, fully embracing who you are without apology, embracing scars as proof of endurance, embracing desires as valid, embracing dreams as achievable. This love within became the foundation from which all other love could flow. It was the spark, the reminder that connection is possible when you first honor your own presence.

Healing had prepared me for connection, teaching me what I deserved, what boundaries were necessary, & what patterns no longer served me. I learned to identify love that nurtures growth, that aligns with values, that enhances rather than diminishes. Toxicity became visible not as an accusation but as insight, guiding me toward spaces, people, & experiences that affirmed my worth. This discernment was vital because love that supports is rare, & love that mirrors the respect we hold for ourselves is even rarer.

Connection is not about perfection. It is about authenticity. It is about presence, intention, & mutual respect. When I allowed myself to be seen fully, without masks, without apologies, I discovered a new kind of intimacy. Vulnerability became a bridge rather than a risk, a language of trust rather than fear. Love revealed itself not only in grand gestures but in quiet attentiveness, in the recognition of each other's struggles & triumphs, in patience & grace extended freely.

Animals continued to teach me about love. Pops & Sebast reminded me that love does not demand performance, that loyalty does not come with conditions, that presence alone can communicate devotion. In their eyes, in their paws, in their quiet companionship, I saw reflection of a love that was unconditional, consistent, & nonjudgmental. These lessons were essential as I navigated human relationships, grounding me in the understanding that love's most powerful expression is often simplicity itself.

Love is not only about receiving; it is profoundly about giving. It requires generosity of spirit, patience, & the willingness to see beyond the immediate self. I learned to balance boundaries with openness, to extend empathy without compromising integrity, & to cultivate compassion without sacrificing agency. Every act of love offered became a statement of strength, a declaration that my heart could remain open despite past hurts, that tenderness & resilience coexist naturally.

Intimacy with another person demanded courage. I carried the weight of past betrayals, of fears once internalized, & of trust that had been fractured. Yet, as strength solidified within me, I discovered the ability to approach relationships not from desperation or avoidance but from clarity & choice. Love became not an escape from self but an extension of self, a space where two individuals can grow, reflect, & build a shared journey without losing individual sovereignty.

Communication became central. Speaking truthfully, listening actively, & honoring emotions were acts of love in themselves. I learned that misunderstandings are not failures, but opportunities for growth, for insight, for deeper connection. Conflict, when navigated consciously, revealed areas for personal evolution & mutual understanding. Love, I realized, thrives not in harmony alone but in the courageous engagement with discomfort, with difference, & with the unknown.

Joy emerged as a companion to love. Shared laughter, playful interactions, & simple presence became indicators of connection, subtle reminders that life can be tender, pleasurable, & fulfilling. I noticed that love is not measured by intensity but by consistency, reliability, & mutual investment. It is present when someone celebrates small victories, offers comfort without expectation, & affirms the essence of your being simply by being present.

Self-love remained paramount. I could not rely solely on external validation because it is fleeting, unpredictable, & external. Love that is dependent on another's approval is unstable, fragile, & conditional. By centering my own worth, celebrating achievements, honoring boundaries, & embracing desires, I created a foundation from which all other love could thrive. It became a lens through which I could assess relationships, ensuring alignment with growth, respect, & shared values.

Love is also transformative. It encourages self-reflection, growth, & the shedding of past fears. It illuminates shadowed areas of the self, revealing unhealed wounds, ingrained patterns, & suppressed desires. True love demands honesty, compassion, & patience. It nurtures the evolution of both partners simultaneously, allowing space for mistakes, learning, & redefinition. Through love, I discovered the power of empathy, the strength in patience, & the grace of mutual understanding.

Fear occasionally surfaces, reminding me of prior trauma, past mistakes, & vulnerabilities. But awakening strength taught me that courage does not eliminate fear; it moves forward despite it. By engaging with love consciously, I cultivated trust in myself, in my instincts, & in my capacity to navigate uncertainty. Love became not a gamble but a deliberate choice, a practice in faith, courage, & presence.

Connection extends beyond romance. Friendship, mentorship, family, & community offer profound love that sustains, inspires, & anchors. I embraced these relationships fully, understanding that reciprocal respect & care are vital to sustaining meaningful bonds. Through shared experiences, mutual support, & emotional honesty, these connections reinforced resilience, encouraged growth, & nurtured the human spirit.

The journey of love after trauma is not linear. It is cyclical, often tentative, & requires ongoing reflection. I discovered that patience is indispensable, allowing space for gradual trust, understanding, & integration of emotional experiences. Boundaries remain essential, acting not as walls but as protective structures that ensure safety, clarity, & the freedom to flourish.

I learned to appreciate the small gestures of love: a shared smile, a gentle touch, a supportive word, a silent presence. These moments, often overlooked, became evidence of connection, intimacy, & genuine regard. Love is cumulative, built from intention, awareness, & repeated acts of care. It thrives when nurtured consistently & honored fully.

Through the conscious cultivation of love, I reclaimed the narrative of my life. Trauma had taught caution, withdrawal, & guardedness, but awakening strength enabled the embrace of intimacy without compromise. Love became a space of empowerment, not dependency, offering joy without relinquishing agency. Each experience, each interaction, each moment of vulnerability reinforced the principle that love is both a gift & a practice, requiring attention, respect, & courage.

In embracing love, I recognized its multifaceted nature. Romantic love, platonic love, familial love, self-love, & universal love intersect, each enriching the other, each offering lessons in trust, patience, & empathy. I learned to celebrate diversity in expressions of affection, understanding that every form of love holds value, meaning, & potential for growth.

Ultimately, love is freedom. Freedom to feel deeply, to act authentically, & to extend compassion without sacrificing identity. Love, after trauma, is reclamation: of joy, of trust, of presence, & of the capacity to connect meaningfully. It is evidence that life continues, that resilience enables intimacy, & that the heart, when honored, can open fully again.

By nurturing love consciously, I discovered that it is not merely a destination but a journey. It requires courage, self-awareness, patience, & consistency. It thrives when aligned with strength, respect, & intentionality. Love illuminates, transforms, & elevates, offering the reminder that connection is possible, joy is attainable, & hearts can heal.

Through love, I integrated strength & vulnerability, courage & tenderness, autonomy & connection. I realized that the love I give, receive, & embody is not only restorative but generative, creating ripples that extend far beyond the immediate, influencing both self & world positively. Love became a compass, guiding decisions, relationships, & actions toward authenticity, fulfillment, & meaningful growth.

Every act of love, small or grand, conscious or intuitive, reinforced the affirmation that I am worthy, I am capable, & I am deserving. Love does not erase the past, but it transforms its lessons into tools for connection, insight, & empowerment. In embracing love, I discovered the profound beauty of choosing to remain open, of trusting life, & of allowing light to enter spaces that once held darkness.

Part Five
Embracing Joy

Joy is not always loud. It is not always explosive or dramatic. Sometimes it is subtle, quiet, tucked into moments we almost overlook, waiting patiently for our awareness to arrive. After surviving trauma, reclaiming strength, & opening ourselves to love, joy becomes not just a feeling but a conscious practice, a daily choice, & a declaration that life can be gentle, expansive, & fulfilling. Embracing joy requires attention, intentionality, & a willingness to notice the small sparks that illuminate our path.

The first whispers of joy came in silence. In the early mornings, with sunlight spilling softly through the windows, I noticed the rhythm of my breath, the warmth of my body, & the way the world continued in its persistent beauty. I recognized that life had not paused despite my pain. Joy was available, quietly waiting to be recognized, not as a reward for surviving, but as an essential companion to resilience. This understanding became foundational, reminding me that pleasure & contentment are not luxuries but vital acts of self-respect.

Animals, ever faithful teachers, continued to guide me. Pops & Sebast offered joy without expectation, demonstrating that delight can be found in the simplest acts: a wagging tail, a playful bark, a shared glance filled with recognition & love. Observing their energy, I remembered the importance of presence, the magic of noticing without judgment, & the power of unguarded delight. Their companionship taught me that joy is less about circumstances & more about perception, less about control & more about openness.

Gratitude became inseparable from joy. I learned to honor both triumphs & struggles, recognizing that each step, no matter how small, contributes to the unfolding of life's beauty. The scars I once perceived as burdens became evidence of survival, & survival became evidence of strength, & strength became fertile ground for happiness. In this reframing, joy was not the absence of hardship but the acknowledgment that beauty persists despite it, that light emerges even in shadowed places, & that laughter, love, & wonder are not only possible but inevitable when nurtured consciously.

I discovered that joy requires courage. It requires stepping into the unknown, taking risks, & allowing ourselves to feel fully. After trauma, fear can become an automatic companion, whispering caution & uncertainty. Joy demands a counterbalance: presence, curiosity, & engagement with life even when hesitation lingers. Choosing happiness is an act of rebellion against past limitations, a statement that we will not be defined solely by pain but by our capacity to thrive, to explore, & to delight in existence.

Community played a crucial role in expanding my joy. Surrounding myself with supportive, uplifting individuals reinforced that happiness is amplified when shared. Connection fosters laughter, inspiration, & mutual celebration. We become mirrors, reflecting not only challenges but also victories. Each shared experience magnifies joy, transforming moments of contentment into lasting memories that anchor the heart in appreciation & presence.

Creativity became another gateway. Writing, painting, reflection, & expression transformed mundane experiences into celebrations of insight, growth, & imagination. Creating allowed the heart to process, release, & convert struggle into beauty. Each piece of work became a testament to survival & an invitation for joy to inhabit space once occupied by fear. This process reminded me that fulfillment is often constructed, not merely discovered, & that engaging with life actively produces its own pleasure, purpose, & sense of accomplishment.

Mindfulness deepened my capacity for joy. Paying attention to sensations, emotions, & surroundings cultivated awareness that pleasure exists in immediacy. Taste, touch, sound, sight, & movement became portals for delight. A warm cup of tea, sunlight on skin, a breeze across the face, the laughter of a friend, or the soft snuggle of a pet became reminders that happiness is not a distant horizon but a living, breathing moment. These small recognitions, repeated consistently, accumulate into a reservoir of contentment & resilience.

Celebrating progress, not perfection, became a mantra. Each victory, regardless of size, reinforced self-worth & fostered optimism. Joy flourishes when we honor incremental growth, acknowledging that life's triumphs are not always monumental but are equally meaningful in cumulative effect. Recognizing our efforts, our courage, & our persistence allows joy to solidify as a reliable companion rather than a fleeting, unpredictable guest.

Playfulness reentered life as an act of liberation. Laughter, spontaneity, & embracing curiosity became reminders that lightness is possible even after hardship. Engaging in activities that spark wonder, creativity, & connection restores energy, opens the heart, & reinforces a sense of aliveness. Play is not trivial; it is a recognition that existence is not only survival but also enjoyment, that embracing delight honors the soul & affirms vitality.

Self-compassion reinforced joy. Accepting ourselves fully, celebrating strengths, & forgiving perceived shortcomings creates internal harmony. This harmony becomes a fertile environment where happiness can flourish. By treating ourselves with kindness, patience, & understanding, we reinforce the notion that we are worthy of pleasure, laughter, & contentment, irrespective of past difficulties or external validation.

Nature reminded me of joy's constancy. Trees, water, sunlight, & sky offered solace & inspiration. Observing natural rhythms, the bloom of flowers, the rise & fall of tides, or the flight of birds instilled awe, grounding, & a sense of wonder. These moments became practices in presence, gratitude, & recognition that joy is woven into the fabric of existence, available to those who pause to observe & honor it.

Joy is also rooted in purpose. Engaging in work, creation, service, & contribution aligns personal effort with meaning, fostering a sense of fulfillment that extends beyond immediate gratification. Purpose illuminates life, provides direction, & transforms routine actions into opportunities for significance. Each contribution, whether grand or modest, becomes a channel for joy, integrating intention with satisfaction, effort with contentment, & action with reward.

Forgiveness opened doors to freedom. Releasing resentment, blame, & attachment to past hurts liberated emotional space, allowing joy to emerge where stagnation once prevailed. Forgiveness is not about condoning actions but reclaiming power, restoring peace, & inviting light. This internal shift transforms the heart, fosters clarity, & creates capacity for positive connection, pleasure, & authentic engagement with life.

Love & joy intertwined seamlessly. The deeper my connections with others & myself became, the more joy expanded, feeding on shared experience, empathy, & understanding. Moments of intimacy, celebration, & emotional resonance reinforced that happiness is rarely solitary; it thrives in exchange, reflection, & collaboration. The heart's capacity for delight grows exponentially when nurtured in relational & personal harmony.

Resilience continued to underpin every experience. Joy is not naive or blind to struggle; it coexists with challenge, uncertainty, & occasional sorrow. Embracing happiness is an act of courage, a commitment to life, & a declaration that our spirit is unyielding. Each experience of delight reinforces strength, offering proof that recovery, growth, & flourishing are possible despite adversity.

Through gratitude, presence, & intentionality, I embraced a life rich in joy. Every breath, interaction, & reflection became an opportunity to notice beauty, extend compassion, & celebrate existence. Joy is not a destination but a path, a series of conscious choices, & a recognition that life, with all its complexity, holds countless opportunities for pleasure, connection, & love.

Ultimately, embracing joy is a reclamation of the self. It affirms resilience, celebrates growth, & honors both struggle & triumph. Joy is a declaration that we are present, capable, & deserving. It is a companion that walks alongside us, a lens through which life's intricacies are illuminated, & a promise that beauty, connection, & happiness can always be cultivated consciously, generously, & fully.

By committing to joy, I recognized that life is abundant, multifaceted, & deeply rewarding. Every moment offers potential for discovery, laughter, & wonder. Joy becomes a lens, a daily choice, & an enduring affirmation that we can thrive, connect, & live fully, even after trauma. It is the culmination of survival, strength, & love—a declaration that life is not only bearable but vibrant, expansive, & luminous.

Closing Reflections & Acknowledgements

As I reach the end of this journey, I pause to breathe in the fullness of all that has been lived, felt, lost, & found again. Writing this book has been more than a process; it has been a conversation with my own heart, with the memories of those I loved, & with the quiet strength that never left me even when I thought it had. Every page carries the echo of a past that shaped me, the pulse of love that sustained me, & the hope that whispers of all that is yet to come.

To my Mum, whose love built the foundations of who I am: your warmth, your courage, & your unwavering care remain with me in every choice I make. Even though your voice is no longer here to guide me aloud, I feel it in every gentle breeze, in every quiet moment of courage, & in the rhythm of my heartbeat. You taught me that love persists beyond absence, beyond time, & beyond fear. I carry you with me always.

To Derry, my foster mum, my anchor in the years after loss: you reminded me that safety can be restored & that trust can be rebuilt when the world feels unkind. Your kindness, patience, & quiet faith in me were miracles that continue to echo in my life. Thank you for showing me that family is sometimes found in those who choose to stay, who see you, & who never turn away.

To Pops, my golden boy, my teacher of unconditional love: you gave me laughter, calm, & courage in ways only a loyal heart can. You taught me devotion without expectation, patience without frustration, & joy without conditions. Even now, your spirit guides Sebast & me, reminding us that love is not limited to time, & that bonds remain eternal when they are true.

To Sebast, my little shadow, my constant companion: you are the reminder that healing is a journey, not a destination. Your gentle trust, your curiosity, & your quiet devotion show me that love continues to grow even when pain has touched the heart. Together we learn, step by step, paw by paw, how to walk forward with courage & gentleness.

To every friend, every reader, & every soul who has taken the time to journey with me through these pages: thank you for listening, for holding space, & for honouring my truth. Your presence matters, even in silence. Your recognition of my story is a gift that continues the cycle of love & understanding that this world so desperately needs.

To the universe that has carried me through storms too vast for words, I am grateful. To the moments of silence, of reflection, of small victories, thank you for showing me that resilience often grows quietly, patiently, & invisibly. To life itself, with all its heartbreaks & miracles, I offer my gratitude for teaching me how to rise again, how to love again, & how to be fully, unapologetically myself.

This book is not just a record of what has happened. It is a celebration of survival, a testament to love, & a dedication to the heart's unyielding capacity to heal. If you take one thing away from these pages, let it be this: love endures, even when it seems impossible, & light can always be found, even in the deepest shadows.

Forever we are. Forever we will be.

With all my heart, gratitude, & love,

Debs

www.ingramcontent.com/pod-product-compliance
Lightning Source LLC
Chambersburg PA
CBHW051253120626
46547CB00014B/1926